PRESTWICH & WHITEFIELD

THROUGH TIME

Paul Hindle and Harry Wilkinson

AMBERLEY

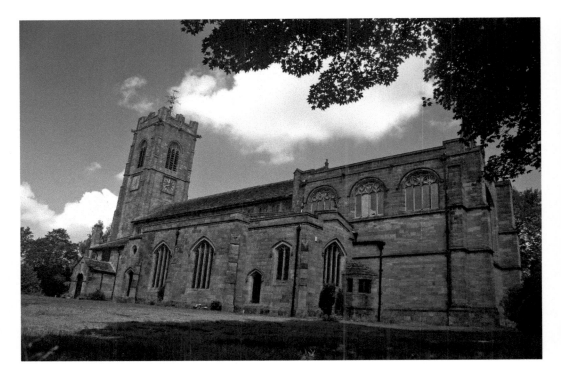

Church of St Mary the Virgin, Prestwich
Prestwich parish church is Grade I listed.

First published 2020

Amberley Publishing
The Hill, Stroud
Gloucestershire, GL5 4EP

www.amberley-books.com

Copyright © Paul Hindle and Harry Wilkinson, 2020

The rights of Paul Hindle and Harry Wilkinson
to be identified as the Authors of this work have
been asserted in accordance with the Copyrights,
Designs and Patents Act 1988.

ISBN 978 1 4456 9946 2 (print)
ISBN 978 1 4456 9947 9 (ebook)

British Library Cataloguing in Publication Data.
A catalogue record for this book is available from
the British Library.

Typeset in 10pt on 13pt Celeste.
Origination by Amberley Publishing.
Printed in the UK.

About the Authors

Paul Hindle

Paul was born in Prestwich and attended Stand Grammar School. He took Geography degrees at Manchester and Salford universities. He lived in Prestwich and Whitefield before moving a few miles away to Ringley. After taking (very) early retirement from being a senior lecturer in Geography at Salford University, he continues to research, write and lecture in various fields of historical geography. His main academic interests are historic maps, roads, canals, the Lake District and towns and roads in medieval England. He has written over a dozen books, including four for Amberley, and commentaries for numerous maps in the Godfrey Edition of early Ordnance Survey maps.

He is editor of *North West Geography*, the e-journal of the Manchester Geographical Society, of which he is honorary secretary (www.mangeogsoc. org.uk), and chairman and editor of the Manchester Bolton & Bury Canal Society (www.mbbcs.org.uk).

Harry Wilkinson

Harry was born in Whitefield and was educated at Stand Grammar School. He graduated in Geography at London University's Queen Mary College. He later studied for professional qualifications in librarianship at Sheffield University. He spent much of his working life in the public libraries of Prestwich and Whitefield. Apart from when studying, and two years' National Service in the RAF, he has lived in the area all his life. His interest in local history stems from meeting proper local historians in the course of his work and realising that if the local libraries didn't try to collect and preserve material of local interest, it could probably be lost forever. He would like to acknowledge the contributions to his learning from Ian Pringle, Ian Pratt and John Wilson.

Rather strangely the two authors lived next door to each other in Whitefield for much of the 1950s and 1960s. And another connection was that Harry's father was the manager of Timpson's in Prestwich (see page 15).

Yates' Map *c.* 1780

William Yates surveyed Lancashire in around 1780, and the map shows a very different landscape. Prestwich has houses around the parish church, and Stand has two halls and a dissenting chapel (DC). There are more houses around Besses and Whitefield, and Lord Grey de Wilton is named as the owner of Heaton House. But Bury New Road and Radcliffe New Road had not then been built. Instead, Bury Old Road led to Besses where it split for Radcliffe and Bury.

Introduction

Prestwich and Whitefield, with a combined population of around 55,000, are affluent suburban areas 5 miles north of Manchester. They have grown together in the space between the towns of Manchester, Salford and Bury. Prestwich was formerly a municipal borough and Whitefield was an urban district, with many local services provided by Lancashire County Council. Both became somewhat reluctant parts of the metropolitan borough of Bury in 1974.

This is an area of poor soils, formed from glacial deposits on top of sandstone rocks. It is mainly flat, except for the cliffs of Springwater Park in the north, and the steep valleys (cloughs) of streams running into the River Irwell to the west.

The name Prestwich comes from the Old English words for 'priests' retreat', a reference to an old religious establishment. It is unclear where Whitefield got its name – possibly a corruption of 'wheatfield', from the practice of laying cloth out in the fields to bleach it white, or because white flowers grew in abundance in the Lilyhill area.

Over the centuries, churches have dominated the scene. St Mary's was the original Prestwich parish church. The tower was built in the late fifteenth century, but the foundation was much earlier, in Norman times. Stand Church, which towers over Whitefield, was built much later, having been a chapel of ease of Prestwich parish church. It was a 'Waterloo' church, funded after the Napoleonic Wars. It was designed by Charles Barry and was consecrated in 1826. Also, historically important is Stand Unitarian Chapel, a dissenters' chapel formed here because it was 5 miles away from any town centre. Stand took its name from the hunting lodge in the medieval Pilkington Park; this covered most of Whitefield.

Transport has been critical in the development of the area. There are two main routes leading north from Manchester: Bury Old Road was the first road to be turnpiked in 1755, followed by Bury New Road in 1826, partly on the line of the Roman road from Manchester to Ribchester. These two roads met at Besses o' th' Barn, named after the old hostelry on the site, which was

4

apparently run by a landlady called Bess! Later, tramlines were laid on these roads. The railway line between Bury and Manchester was opened in 1879, passing through Prestwich and Whitefield, and was critical for their development. It survived the Beeching cuts and has now become a busy part of the Metrolink commuter tram system. The M60 motorway has now divided the townships where previously roads joined them together.

Because the land was relatively poor for agriculture, much of it remained in large estates, owned by old families such as that of de Prestwich, de Radcliffe, de Holland and the Langleys. One example is Heaton Park, which was the seat of the Egerton family (later the Earls of Wilton), before it was bought by Manchester Corporation in 1902 and turned into a public park. Eventually these estates were broken up and rich merchants built their large houses there. Later the grounds of these big houses were sold off for estates of smaller housing. The last big housing development was the building of the Hillock estate in Whitefield for Manchester Corporation.

In 1847, one large estate was bought to be developed into Prestwich Lunatic Asylum. The area was thought to be much healthier than the polluted inner parts of Manchester. It became one of the largest mental hospitals in the country, with its own farm, church, football and cricket pitches. It was probably the area's largest employer. Several of the specialist units still exist, hidden behind a supermarket. This replaced most of the hospital when 'care in the community' became the policy; over the years, many nurses were recruited from Ireland. The Irish influence is still noticeable, as is the Jewish influence. The area has a large Jewish community and contains several burial grounds and synagogues.

It is thought that, because much of the area was split into these large estates, and their rich owners did not want factories, industrial development did not take place. Several small textile mills, some using the waters of the cloughs, did operate, but never on the large scale of neighbouring towns. They have now all gone. Even the Halls sweet factory, which once made Whitefield famous worldwide for 'Halls Mentho-Lyptus' no longer exists.

In the past, the village centres were able to support many small shops, pubs and places of entertainment. With the growth of supermarkets, and the great expansion of car ownership, many have been forced to close. They have been unable to compete with larger towns. This has altered the appearance of the village centres; many of the old buildings are now occupied by restaurants and takeaways, offices and residential use. Prestwich and Whitefield have become residential suburbs.

Motorway

The M62 (now the M60) was opened in 1970–71, along the line of the former Yorkshire Road, which had a wide grass strip down the middle, clearly intended for a wide trunk road. The motorway was much wider and deeper, and many houses were demolished. There is what is effectively a double-deck bridge with the Metrolink line and Bury Old Road crossing the motorway. The motorway clearly separates Whitefield on the left from Prestwich on the right.

Prestwich Parish Church

Prestwich is derived from the Old English for 'priests' retreat' and St Mary's Church was at its original centre. Although Prestwich is not mentioned in Domesday Book, the church has Norman origins. The 86-foot red-sandstone tower was built in the late fifteenth century by the Earl of Derby; its bells were broadcast nationally to mark the victory at El Alamein in 1942. The chancel, vestry and organ chamber were built in 1889. The church has been seen in episodes of Coronation Street.

Prestwich Church

Prestwich Church

St Mary's Church and the Church Inn

The inn, originally named The Ostrich, dates back to the early seventeenth century. Over the years, it has been the centre of many of the town's festivities. The ancient 'rushcart' processions used to end in front of the inn, but they were stopped in 1840 because they often ended in drunkenness. Like many old pubs, the Church Inn is reputed to be haunted; the ghost of Old Tom is said to move barrels around in the cellar.

Prestwich Hospital

The County Lunatic Asylum was opened in 1851, the site chosen for its general salubrity. Originally planned for 500 patients, it grew greatly in size, and at its peak, the hospital had over 3,000 inmates. It was almost self-sufficient, with its own farm, gas and electricity supplies, fire station and sporting facilities. The patients and staff gave the town a certain ambience! Now only specialist units are left on the site, as a supermarket and housing have covered much of the old asylum grounds.

South Lodge

The lodge was on Clifton Road, which was the packhorse road to Clifton. Further down the road the Asylum Annexe was built in 1881, well away from the main buildings. It was planned to house 1,100 inmates. Care in the Community became the new way of treatment in the 1980s and more patients were now treated outside the hospital. The site still has a secure unit. There was a local saying that 'going to Prestwich' meant going mad.

Tower Buildings

The old shopping centre of Prestwich was demolished to make way for Prestwich Co-op's main department store, the Tower Buildings. This was officially opened in 1926 and extended to include the food hall in 1960. The Co-op also acquired the former Savoy Dance Hall at the rear, which became the focus of the Co-op's considerable educational activities and was also the main restaurant in Prestwich. The Co-op had a turnover of over £1 million in 1961, but the Tower Buildings closed in 1987.

Railway and Naturalist

Following the demolition of the Tower Buildings, the whole area was redeveloped. New commercial premises front the main road, and new flats tower over the Longfield Centre. The Railway and Naturalist pub has remained. Built in 1850, it was first known as the Naturalist's Inn, after the famous local botanists held their meetings here until the First World War. In the 1870s the local railway was being constructed, and the thirsty railway workers made it their drinking place.

Bury New Road

The old view was taken from the corner of Rectory Lane (it is now the opening to the Longfield Precinct). The building with shops behind the tram standard was the old Albion Inn, which closed in 1922, but the signage remains. Prestwich Methodist Church can be seen in the distance. A recent scheme has introduced parking spaces and landscaping with trees to this main road.

Bury New Road

The shops are little changed, but the National School, designed by Alfred Waterhouse, with its clock tower was demolished in 1983. The Labour Exchange in various guises has gone to Rectory Lane. All the signs of increased road traffic are in the recent picture – road markings, lights for the crossing, queues of cars.

Timpson's Shoe shop
Timpson's shoe shop was a branch of the family-owned chain. In the 1940s there were at least three shoe shops in Prestwich; now there are none. In the manager's cubicle, in the centre of the shop, there was a trapdoor that led to the basement, which was used to do some shoe repairs, as well as serving as the staff dining room. Above the shop was the Victoria Club, a gentleman's dining and social club. The club is now a tattoo parlour called 'Sorry Mum'!

Clarks Hill

This quiet road alongside the Red Lion pub was part of the old route to Prestwich and to St Mary's Church from Bury Old Road before Bury New Road was turnpiked in 1826. It got its name because it went across the parish clerk's meadow. The charm of this ancient lane was lost following a Compulsory Purchase Order in 1971. It now contains flats and sheltered housing.

Conservative Club

Prestwich Conservative Club was founded in 1874 and moved into these premises in 1880. By the 1950s, the building needed expensive repairs, and the club decided to move to a property already owned on the other side of Church Lane called Spring Bank. This had been used as a base for their tennis club and had large terraced gardens. The original club building was bought by Lancashire County Council as an adult education centre, but it is now used for commercial purposes.

Church Institute & Mens Club, Prestwich.

Church Institute

The 'Stute' opened in 1902, partly financed by funds raised for Queen Victoria's Diamond Jubilee. It was a social club for men aged eighteen or over, of St Mary's parish. As well as hosting a library, there was a meeting room, a games room and a bar. Not a lot has changed, but it has lost its bowling green, which was sold for housing.

Plaza Cinema

The cinema opened as the Picturedrome in 1911, and was renamed as the Plaza in 1930 when it was fitted with 'the most expensive and finest talkie system in the world'. After it closed in 1959, it first became a bingo hall, then a warehouse and finally an auction house. The building was demolished in 1999 to make way for an apartment block.

St Mary's Park

The park was opened by Lord Derby in 1931 with large crowds present. The flower gardens were laid out in geometric patterns on former glebe land called Church Fields. There was a bandstand on a grassy knoll and a shelter with a veranda and seating. Lovely views were enjoyed of the Clough, Prestwich Park and St Mary's Church.

St Ann's Road and Prestwich Park
This wooded area, between the Clough and Butterstile Lane, was developed as a quality private estate from 1851. It was laid out with North and South Lodges. Originally five large villas were built with views over the Clough and St Mary's Church, on what is now St Ann's Road.

Prestwich Library

This library was opened in 1933 as part of Lancashire County Library's drive to make libraries accessible to everyone. In the entrance it had a counter with turnstiles; the books in the main lending area were kept on unusual step-like shelves. It closed in 1972 when the library in the Longfield Centre opened. It is now the theatre of the Prestwich Amateur Dramatic and Operatic Society (PADOS). The War Memorial has been moved to the gardens in front of the building.

Rectory Lane

This once quiet lane was part of the route linking the communities of Heaton Park and Prestwich Village. The original rectory, a very large building called the Deyne, stood where Rectory Avenue (the first road off to the left) is now. The bottom of the hill was filled in and the road widened in 1925. At around the same time, the Dingle was filled in and levelled to form St Mary's playing fields.

Prestwich Town Hall.

Prestwich Town Hall

Prestwich became an Urban District in 1897; the offices were moved to this building in 1920. It had been a mansion called Bent Hill, built in the 1850s for a rich merchant. Originally it had 17 acres of grounds, but most of this was soon used for council housing. Prestwich became a municipal borough in 1939. The Town Hall was no longer needed after Prestwich became part of Bury in 1974, and the building has been tastefully converted into very nice apartments.

Savings Centre

At the busy junction of Hilton Lane and Bury New Road stands this very striking art deco building. During the Second World War, saving was encouraged to pay for the war, and Savings Centres were set up. Children were asked to put their pocket money into Savings Stamps. Prestwich sponsored a submarine, the *Utmost*, which was lost in 1943. The building is now an attractive block of shops and apartments.

Sedgley Park Methodist Church

The lodge to Sedgley Hall once occupied this site, and the trees in the background are a reminder of the gardens of the mansions of Sedgley Park. In 1913 a hall was built for dual use as a church and Sunday school. As the congregation grew, more room was needed. A new church was built alongside, and this opened in 1940. In the 1990s, it was found to require unaffordable repairs. The church closed in 1992 and has been replaced by a synagogue.

Bury New Road, Sedgley Park

The Odeon cinema is on the right of this view from the Salford boundary looking towards Sedgley Park. It started as the Astoria in 1931 and became the Odeon in 1937, closing in 1961. It was also a dance hall and a nightclub and the site is now a Lidl store. The George Hotel on the opposite side had a bowling green used in major tournaments. This has now disappeared under a car park.

Heathlands

Heathlands was the name of the Victorian mansion which had been the home of Mr Athanasius Demetriadi. He was the last of a line of Greek merchant families that had settled in Prestwich since the 1850s. He died in 1963, and the site has been redeveloped as Heathlands Village, a highly regarded Jewish nursing and residential home.

Prestwich Railway Station

The railway has been crucial to the development of Prestwich since its arrival in 1879. The station had booking offices at the ground-level entrance, and up the stairs at platforms level there were waiting rooms and shelter from the distinctive canopy. A much longer platform was required for the trains, which were replaced by trams in 1992.

Prestwich Cricket Club

The cricket club was founded in 1840 and played in several locations before buying the current site on the Heys in 1913. It had been a rough meadow, but the members levelled it and culverted a stream to form the cricket square and tennis courts, and bowling green. Some land was sold for housing, and in 2010 this has helped to finance the new pavilion and function rooms.

Kirkhams

The big house on the corner of Derby Road was built in 1733 by Thomas Kirkham, a cotton manufacturer, from which the area got its name. Just out of sight round the bend was Bentley bridge, which carried the railway line over the road. It was named after the Bentley Brewery attached to the nearby Coach and Horses pub. It was also known as the 'Cephos' bridge after the advert for the powders (a cure for winter ills) on the side.

Polefield, Prestwich. PWH.10

Polefield

Bury Old Road has very wide pavements in this area, enough to have a separate service road to these shops. At the north end is a popular fish and chip shop, advertised as 'The Home of the Jumbo Cod'! Behind is the Polefield housing estate, built mainly on the grounds of the old Polefield Hall, a large house that was used as a hospital in the First World War.

Bury Old Road, Holyrood

The bank on the corner of St Margaret's Road is now the Royal Bank of Scotland, though at first it was a branch of Williams Deacons Bank. The shop at the other end of the row is 'Transformation', a firm which achieved some notoriety when it first opened selling clothes for cross-dressers. The land alongside was at one time the Holyrood Nursing Home, then Barlows Removals, and now housing.

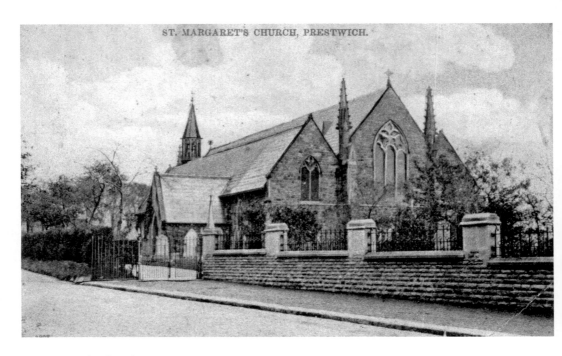

St Margaret's Church

The Earl of Wilton donated the land for the building of this church in 1849. It opened in 1851 to seat 500 parishioners in the Holyrood area. It kept its open plan until 1920, when a carved oak chancel screen was installed in memory of Joseph Holt, killed at Gallipoli. He was the son of Sir Edward Holt of the brewery family who lived at Woodthorpe. It reverted to the open plan after a serious fire in 1985.

Simister

Simister was until recently very much a rural village. It was named after James Simister, a farmer and landowner who built a house there in 1738. The lane was part of the old route from Prestwich to Oldham, in the times when Oldham was part of the parish of Prestwich. Many of the cottages have been demolished, but the Farmers Arms remains in the centre of the village.

Same Yet
The inn in Simister got
its name in around 1885;
it is said that the inn had
its sign ruined in a storm.
The sign writer asked the
landlord what he wanted
on the new sign. He replied
'same yet', meaning 'the
same as before', but the
sign writer took him
literally! The original name
was probably the Bulls
Head, after the crest of the
de Radcliffe family.

Heaton Park Station

The first trains of the Lancashire and Yorkshire Railway ran through Prestwich in 1879. The Earl of Wilton did not want the view spoiled. He insisted that the line went underground across his parkland, and therefore a 713-yard tunnel was built. The first trains were steam trains, and these continued for goods such as coal, but electric passenger trains started running in 1916. The line is now part of the Metrolink tram system.

Bury Old Road

Bury Old Road was the first road to be turnpiked in Prestwich, in 1755. The big wall of Heaton Park dominated the scene on this part of the road. The Station Lodge, sometimes called the Church Lodge, guarded the entrance to the park opposite Heaton Park railway station, where the railway emerged from the tunnel under the park. The former Turf Tavern is said to have been named after the horse racing that took place in the park.

Ostrich Hotel

The hotel takes its name from the crest of the Coke family, who were the Lords of the Manor of Prestwich. It was in this hotel that Thomas Coke sold off his lands in Prestwich in 1777 in order to concentrate on his Norfolk estates. On the far side of Ostrich Lane there was a tearoom with a distinctive spire. It was a place to buy drinks in the days when a day trip out to Heaton Park was popular.

Holy Law Synagogue

Jews who had arrived in the Cheetham Hill area in the nineteenth century formed the Holy Law congregation in 1865. The Jewish cemetery in Prestwich village had opened as early as 1840. As more and more Jewish people came to live in Prestwich, the Holy Law joined up with the Sedgley Park congregation to build this new synagogue in Prestwich in 1933. It was on the site of Howcaster Cottage, a house on Bury Old Road.

Heaton House

Heaton Park was bought by Manchester Corporation from the Earl of Wilton in 1902. Heaton House, designed by James Wyatt in 1772, was the centrepiece of the estate. The Egerton family had lived in Heaton since 1684, and as they had grown rich, the estate was developed into a grand country seat, with farm, stables and gardens, all enclosed behind a high brick wall. Many children will remember sitting on the lions at the front of the house. The house is Grade I listed.

Heaton Park Gates 883

Hunt's Series

Grand Lodge

The main gates to Heaton Park on Sheepfoot Lane were built in 1807 – a grand estate had to have a grand entrance. Behind this entrance was the racecourse, where the lake is now. The races were started in 1827 but proved too popular for the gentry. The races finished in 1839 and were transferred to Aintree.

Boating lake

The boating lake was constructed in 1913. Manchester Corporation altered the park to provide recreation for the public. It was the biggest municipal park in the country. The corporation built the lake, and a miniature railway to make access easier. The house was used for art exhibitions and tearooms. There was a bandstand where the regular concerts proved very popular.

Heaton Park, Manchester.

Boating Lake

The park was hugely popular as an accessible green space near the very crowded housing of Manchester and Salford. Many people will have had their first experience of rowing on water there, using the different types of boats, but landing on the islands was forbidden. The Heaton Belle launch could take up to 100 visitors at a time on a cruise round the lake.

Façade of Old Town Hall in Heaton Park, Manchester.

Town Hall Façade

The Colonnade dates to 1822, when it was a striking part of Manchester's first Town Hall on King Street. As Manchester grew, larger premises were needed, and it was replaced by the new Town Hall in 1877. The façade was reassembled stone by stone in Heaton Park in 1912, around the same time as the opening of the lake. It is currently fenced off from the public, as its condition is dangerous.

Heaton Park Golf Course

The Corporation also provided sports facilities in the park; the golf course was opened in 1911. It has hosted many prestigious events over the years and was voted the best municipal golf course in 2005. There is also a pitch and putt course. Some bowling greens were constructed especially for the Commonwealth Games when they were held in Manchester in 2002. There are also several football pitches in the park. The old clubhouse has been totally rebuilt lower down the hill.

Prestwich Clough

The stream in this steep-sided valley drains parts of Prestwich. The council was given 9 acres of this valley land by George Gardner and they also bought 13 acres from him for £2,000, in order to preserve it as a public space, and prevent further house building. In May 1906, the Prestwich Band led a procession to open the Clough to the public. The old Engine Cottage building can be seen on the left. This became the site of the first refreshment rooms.

Prestwich Clough

Previously, the Clough had been oak woodland, which had been grazed by cattle. Now it became an area where the public could walk and enjoy the scenery. The council provided seating and prettified the rustic bridge, and even built a bandstand. Much replanting was carried out. Some effort was put into channelling the stream, which at one time had been badly polluted. The Clough remains a popular place to stroll.

PRESTWICH CLOUGH, MANCHESTER.

Prestwich Clough

At one time, there was a dyeworks at the lower end of the Clough. This was owned by the Buckley family, who lived in a house, called 'Prestwich Clough', sheltered by a plantation of beech trees. Prestwich Clough and Mere Clough were places of study for local naturalists, who became famous nationally and left their name in the Railway and Naturalist inn.

49

Refreshment Rooms, Prestwich Clough

Clough Tearooms

The first refreshment rooms were in the converted Old Engine Cottage; this was demolished and these tearooms were built on the site. They were run for years by the Grimshaw ladies. The size of these purpose-built tearooms indicates the popularity of the park as a recreational attraction. In days not so long ago, going for a walk was one of the few options for a Sunday afternoon.

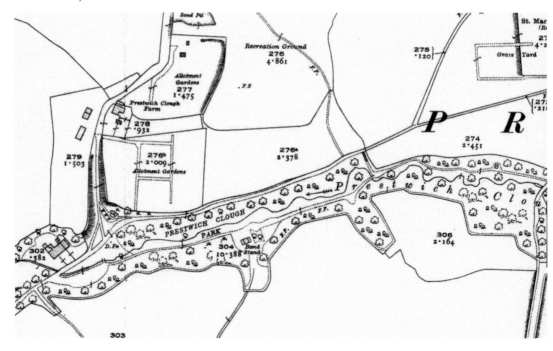

Mere Clough

Bradley Brook is the stream in this clough which runs down to Dams Head and to the Irwell at Red Rocks. It has been the boundary between Prestwich and Whitefield, and 'mære' is an Old English word for a boundary. This was a favourite haunt of the local naturalists. Where the stream splits, there is the 'Ox Gap', a reference to the old packhorse track to Liverpool which crossed the Irwell at Bradley Ford near Red Rocks.

ASYLUM CLOUGH, PRESTWICH.

Asylum Clough

Asylum Clough is another name for Mere Clough. It forms the boundary between the asylum land and Philips Park. A beauty spot in the past, it was later a great playground for lads who found their way there under the Seven Arches of the Philips Park Road viaduct. There were stories of patients who had been found hanging from trees to add spice to their wanderings!

The Park, Prestwich   H. Allen, Prestwich

Philips Park

Robert Philips bought the estate in 1798. The mansion was completed in 1830, and was known simply as 'The Park, Prestwich'. On the death of the last of the Philips family, it became a public park under the joint control of Prestwich and Whitefield councils. The house was demolished in 1950. Later the stables and outbuildings were converted into a nightclub. The thatched cottage was built as the original entrance lodge to the estate, but it was lost when the motorway was constructed.

5300   THE THATCHED COTTAGE, PHILLIPS PARK, PRESTWICH

53

CONSERVATORY & FRONT BORDER – PHILIPS'S PK

Conservatory

The conservatory was set in beautiful gardens. Mass bedding planting was a colourful feature at the foot of the wall that hid the stable buildings. In front of the conservatory was a lily pond. In later years this was often full of frogspawn and tadpoles. Inside there was a bronze fountain. Unfortunately, the building has been the object of vandalism, and has lost its former glory.

North Lodge

This lodge was built in around 1911. Philips Park Road was constructed in 1852. The road made the park more accessible from the main road, and also provided a link to the railway at Molineux Brow. The bridge carrying the road over Mere Clough eventually became dangerous through lack of maintenance and was blown up as part of a Territorial Army exercise in 1965. The danger was not appreciated by the lads who were reputed to have cycled along the parapet!

South Lodge

Dams Head Lodge was the south lodge of the park and was built around the same time as the thatched cottage. It overlooked the millpond, which was one of three ponds supplying water to Bunkers Hill dyeworks. The lodge, despite having no services, continued to be occupied well into the 1960s (sometimes by a lady who ran the café and claimed to be a witch) but was demolished in 1974.

Grass Walk

This steep feature of the gardens led up to the Garden Temple at the top, which houses a marble statue. This reflected the considerable Italianate influence on the gardens of the park. The grass walk was lined with bright flowers, backed up by rhododendrons and azaleas on both sides. Upkeep of the park has suffered from the financial restraints of recent years and it shows.

Drinkwater Park

On the skyline can be seen the chimneys of Prestwich Hospital. In the middle distance was the Drinkwater Park Farm and the Prestwich Sewage Works. The curving lake was part of the landscaping around Irwell House, the mansion of the Drinkwater estate, later used as an isolation hospital. The lake became heavily polluted, especially from the magnesium works across the river at Clifton Junction during the war.

River Irwell

The main span of the 'Thirteen Arches' carried the Lancashire and Yorkshire Railway over the river, with a span of 96 feet and a height of 80 feet. This line opened in 1846 and was closed in the Beeching cuts in 1966. Beyond is Clifton Aqueduct, which carried the Manchester Bolton & Bury Canal across the river, opened in 1796. Because of tree growth, it is impossible now to replicate this view, so the modern photograph is taken in reverse from the aqueduct.

Red Rocks

Photographed in 1888, the children were playing in the waters of the Bradley Brook, the stream which drains Mere Clough. It meets the River Irwell at Red Rocks, near Bradley Ford. This was one of the few places where the river has cut through the glacial drift cover to reveal the underlying sandstone rock. It was later covered in industrial waste but has now been cleaned up. The canal towpath on the other side of the river gives this modern peaceful view.

Rhodes Lock and The Dingle?

This remote lock on the Manchester Bolton & Bury Canal was built in the 1790s. It was used for recreation by the Agecroft Rowing Club between 1860 and 1904. The canal went out of use here in 1936. The Dingle was a deep gully in the area of land between Rectory Lane and Bury New Road, which was filled in the 1930s to create St Mary's playing fields. But the scene pictured looks suspiciously like Ox Gap in Mere Clough. Did the printer get it wrong?

Prestwich Hills Reservoir

In 1867, Manchester Corporation started building the reservoir at Prestwich Hills. The reservoir was needed so that a head of water could be provided for the rapidly growing local area. Before demolition, the Reservoir Keeper's house and a cast-iron crane were features of the area. The site was sold to Barratts for housing in 1984.

Stand Church, Whitefield

The Grade I listed All Saints' Church was designed by Charles Barry in 1822. Some fifteen years later he started on the Houses of Parliament. It was built with a grant from a fund of £1 million provided from Parliament following the victory at the Battle of Waterloo. The land was given by Lord Derby, and the Earl of Wilton laid the foundation stone in 1822; consecration took place in 1826. Recently the building has been cleaned, and its pinnacles reduced in size.

Ringley Road, Stand.

Stand Church from Ringley Road

The dramatic outline of Stand Church on its elevated position can be seen for miles around, notably from the westbound M60. The churchyard was extended towards Ringley Road in the First World War. Ringley Road has changed greatly from a road with only one house, Wallfield, on its length to Stand Lane. It is now filled on both sides with some of the most expensive houses in the area.

Top o' th' Stand

One place called 'Top o' th' Stand' was the now busy junction of Higher Lane, Dales Lane, Ringley Road and Church Lane. Overlooking it, in its peaceful garden, the Cenotaph can be found, inscribed with the names of the fallen in the two World Wars. How the pace of life has changed. Who would sit under a fingerpost in the middle of this junction now?

Church Lane

Large Victorian houses line the road up to the church. A small park was created on the left. One of the big houses has been converted into a nursing home. Another became Whitefield Preparatory School before recently becoming a residence again. Next to it is Whitefield Bowling Club, which is probably the oldest sporting organisation in the town. At the top of the road is the Rectory, a former farmhouse converted by Charles Barry in around 1830.

Stand Grammar School

Stand Grammar School was founded under the will of Henry Siddall in 1688, and at first was housed in premises belonging to Stand Chapel. Clive of India was a pupil. Lancashire County Council took it over and this building was opened in 1913. It was a mixed day school until the Girls' Grammar School (now Philips High School) opened in 1936. The school became part of Bury College. The buildings were demolished in 2001, and housing was built on the site.

Dales Lane

Dales Lane was still a quiet country lane until Radcliffe New Road was made in 1860. Before that Stand Lane was the main route to Radcliffe. In the distance the railway bridge can just be seen and further down on the right was the original Goats Gate pub. Just before the bridge were the outbuildings of The Dales, which were demolished between the wars for housing.

The Dales

The Dales was bought by Nathaniel Philips in 1780. He had been made rich by his family firm of smallware manufacturers, J and N Philips. The mansion stood in extensive grounds, which stretched as far as Chapelfield. In 1904 Stand Golf Club was formed, and a course laid out in the grounds. The house was used as the clubhouse at first, but a new clubhouse was built on the site of the demolished mansion in 1921.

Dales Lodge

This building was originally the entrance lodge to The Dales. The driveway is roughly where Ashbourne Grove now is and led to the big house. Through the gates was the junction of Ringley Road and Higher Lane. The fence separated The Dales estate from the golf course. It is difficult to relate the rural scene to the current position on the very busy crossroads.

Whitefield Railway Station

It was not till 1879 that the Lancashire and Yorkshire Railway came to Whitefield, and the station on Bury New Road was built. There were entrances to the sidings on both sides of the station. In 1916 the line was electrified using the third rail system. At street level, the premises were spacious, with the booking offices to the left, ticket booth in the centre, and luggage and parcel collection areas to the right.

Whitefield Railway Station

The station had a multi-pitched roof and at platform level, facilities such as toilets and waiting rooms heated by coal. The first electric carriages had doors only at the ends, and some seats which were reversible; in the 1960s they were replaced by ones with many more doors. The platforms have been reduced in size, as Metrolink trams are not as long as the trains.

Bury New Road
The bank across Bury New Road was built by Maxwell and Tuke (more famous for designing Blackpool Tower) in 1883; it became a Barclays Bank. There are apartments above the bank and it is currently an Italian restaurant. On the right is the Church Inn, which once achieved fame for its eccentric landlord, who had refused to serve pints to women, and refused to accept the 50p coin which celebrated the entry into the Common Market.

Church Inn

The Church Inn was built in 1830 and it changed its name to Church Inn and Railway Hotel when the railway came in 1879. After extensions and alterations at the turn of the century it reverted to its old name. The inn was demolished almost overnight to make way for the supermarket, and the fine wooden panelling and fixtures were lost. Steam trams started to run from Bury in 1883. They were very noisy and were replaced by electric trams in 1903.

Junction of Radcliffe and Bury New Roads

The Derby Buildings, built in 1896, stood in the middle of this junction. They were at one time the first telephone exchange and then a Home Guard station in the last war. The Co-op store was next to the Derby Hotel on the left. The hotel dates back to the 1860s when Radcliffe New Road was built. It is now one of the many Whitefield pubs that have been converted into eating places.

Radcliffe New Road

There is a lot of activity in this old view, with apparent complete disregard for the open-top tram arriving. The poster in the shop is advertising the Nelson's Centenary, which dates the photo as 1905, 100 years after Trafalgar. The posts were for the overhead tram wires – after the tramlines closed in 1934, the posts were left in position and converted for street lighting. The shop was a newsagent's until recently, but is now yet another eating place.

Radcliffe New Road

The new road was constructed in 1860. The tram to Radcliffe obscures the view of the relatively new housing on Radcliffe New Road. It also obscures the building that was Whitefield Snack Bar– it has been various restaurants over the years and is currently an Italian *cucina*. The chimney of Mathers mill on the far side of Bury New Road is just visible, as are the backs of houses on Bury New Road at the beginning of Lily Hill Street.

The Uplands

This large house was built in 1854, and was owned by a succession of wealthy businessmen, such as John Wild and John Fletcher, both owners of papermaking firms. Whitefield was a much nicer and healthier place to live than places closer to their factories in Radcliffe and Kearsley. The old building was used as a health clinic, prior to the construction of a purpose-built health centre nearby. The proud owner is pictured looking out over what later became Whitefield tennis courts.

Stand Cricket Club

Stand Church and the houses of Hamilton Road form the backdrop to the ground. The large tennis pavilion indicates the popularity of the sport in past times. The pavilion has now gone, as have the club's tennis courts. The bench seating under the neat hedge was often full of spectators, especially when Stand were playing the local sides, Unsworth and Prestwich. The entrance on Hamilton Road had a kiosk where a club member acted as doorman and collected the entry fees.

STAND CRICKET GROUND

Stand Cricket Club

The cricket pavilion with its back to Higher Lane was erected in 1888. The old bar in the corner was built some years later. After the bar was moved to the main pavilion, it has been used as tearooms, tennis changing rooms and now the scorebox. The large house on the horizon was called The Beeches. It was the home of John Ragdale, a prominent member of society who was commemorated in the name of 'houses' at both grammar schools.

TENNIS COURTS, WHITEFIELD.

Whitefield Tennis Courts

The tennis courts were opened in 1925, along with a miniature golf course and surrounding gardens. The semicircular alcoves under the shrubbery lining Hamilton Road were ideal secluded spots for watching tennis being played. Stand Cricket and Tennis Club's courts were at the rear of the pavilion. This had a veranda and was patrolled by the keeper, who collected payments and ensured that times were not exceeded.

Whitefield Tennis Courts
After the First World War in 1921, this area was purchased by public subscription and presented to Whitefield Council for a War Memorial. The fact that it is a memorial is marked by a small granite stone at the Hamilton Road entrance to the gardens. The shale courts have been replaced by landscaped gardens and a children's playground. Part of the land was leased to Stand Cricket and Tennis Club for as long as sport was played there.

Besses Toll Bar

The toll bar was erected by the turnpike trust in 1827 at the junction of Bury New Road and Bury Old Road. The clock tower and Gothic architecture made it a very striking building; it was demolished in 1881. Behind it was the Stone Pale Tavern, which later became the Junction Hotel. Between 1952 and 1963 the landlord of the Junction was Harry Allen, Britain's last official executioner.

Besses O' Th' Barn, Whitefield

Besses o' th' Barn Inn

Below is the rear view of the pub which gave its name to the district. Reputedly, the inn, kept by a lady called Bess, was near a barn, which served as a local landmark. Its real name may have been the Dog Inn or the Bowling Green, but it became officially the Besses o' th' Barn Inn in 1821. It was demolished in 1939 and an ambulance station has since been built on the site.

Robin Hood and Bay Horse

The Robin Hood stood on Higher Lane at Besses junction from 1874 to 1935. It was opposite the old Co-op building next to the old Jewish Burial ground, near the Whitefield Brewery further up the road. The Bay Horse was just a little further up Higher Lane, almost directly opposite the brewery. It was built around 1870 and was open until 1952. It then became a social club and later a weightlifting and judo club before it was demolished in 1965.

Masons Arms

The last version of the Masons Arms was built in around 1902. There had been a beerhouse called the Freemasons Arms on the site since the sixteenth century. The masonic connection has been preserved in the carvings on the pillars by the front entrance. The original pub faced towards Pinfold Lane and was on the land which is now the car park. The building now houses a pâtissier and chocolatier.

1869. Bury New Road, Whitefield.

Red King and Bury New Road

The area round this crossroads was known as Four Lane Ends. The Red King pub was relocated in 1885 to its present site after Moss Lane was realigned to go over the new railway. Besses o' th' Barn Band had rehearsal rooms in a building at the rear of the Red King. The pub is now a quantity surveyor's office; the inset shows the terracotta milestone. It is interesting to see so many of the shops with their blinds out. Was it sunnier in those days?

Town Hall

Hidden by the trees was a house called Underley. This became the Town Hall after Whitefield Urban District Council bought it in 1933 and moved their offices there from Elms Street. They removed the wall and enabled the public to access the landscaped gardens. These featured a small lake with an island, and seats to enjoy the peaceful surroundings. After Bury Metropolitan Borough took over in 1974, the building fell into disuse and disrepair. Only the façade now remains.

Pinfold Lane

This picture shows the junction with Park Lane and Higher Lane. Whereas Pinfold Lane was made up with setts, Park Lane, with the exception of the first few hundred yards, remained a muddy lane until the surge in housebuilding made a decent surface necessary in the 1960s. Stand Grammar School for Girls opened on the corner in 1936. It is now Philips High School.

Higher Lane

Higher Lane is one of the oldest roads in Whitefield on the main route to Radcliffe. It partially follows the line of the Roman road from Manchester to Ribchester. The buildings on the right were outbuildings of Park Hill, and they were demolished in the 1960s to widen the road. Park Hill became a private school for a time and was also demolished for housing in the 1960s.

WHITEFIELD PARK

Whitefield Park

The land for Whitefield Park was donated in 1890 by Alfred Grundy, a rich lawyer who lived at Underley on Pinfold Lane. More land was given by Mark Fletcher and Sons Ltd for bowling greens, alongside which Whitefield Council had a depot and centre for their gardeners. Their place has been taken by a car park and multi-purpose ball zone. The pond with its ducks and bandstand were very popular features in their day.

Whitefield Park.

Whitefield Park

Stand Church, the railway station and the large Victorian houses on Bury New Road could be seen over the lawns of the park. The fountain on the island in the pond was replaced by birdcages, but vandals caused the removal of the birds and the closure of the paddling pool. The growth of the trees and shrubs has completely changed the appearance of the park. The 1907 map shows the size of the development of the centre of Whitefield at that time.

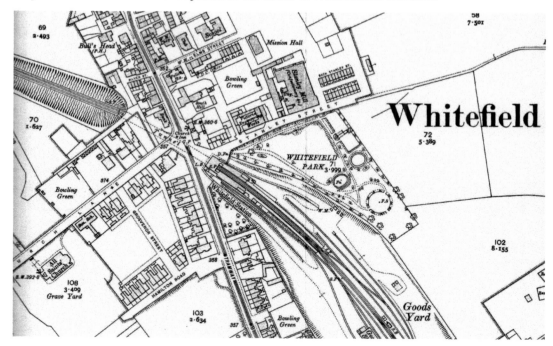

Park Lane School

The school was founded by Robert Needham Philips of The Park in 1847; fifty-six children were enrolled there in 1848. The building was extended in 1878 and 1882 and it changed its name to Whitefield Park Lane British School in 1892. The school closed in 1920 and it was converted into a synagogue in 1959. It was demolished to make way for the new synagogue in 1969. The sandhills at the back provided a great playground for generations of Whitefield children.

Stanley Road

The sweets factory of Hall Bros was started in 1899 and in the 1960s employed around 250 staff, but there was a disastrous fire in 1964. The factory was rebuilt but production was moved to a new factory in Radcliffe. Its famous 'Mentho-Lyptus' sweets are no longer made here. The Fitton's Savoy factory also produced sweets in Whitefield. At the top of the road, Whitefield bus station was built in the 1930s, partly as a scheme to reduce unemployment.

Unitarian Chapel

There has been a dissenting congregation at Stand since 1662; the first chapel was built in 1693. Unitarianism was introduced in 1789 and the first chapel was replaced in 1818. This was destroyed by fire after being hit by an incendiary bomb in 1940. The present chapel, designed in New England style, was built after the end of the war, and opened in 1955.

Stand Old Hall

There have been several old halls in Stand. One was situated at the top of Stand Lane. A building used as a barn is thought to have been part of the last Stand Hall, which was built in the seventeenth century. The roof of this hall collapsed in 1955, and the rest was demolished ten years later. The hall pictured here was called Stand Old Hall and was built in the nineteenth century further up Ringley Road, as indicated on the map.

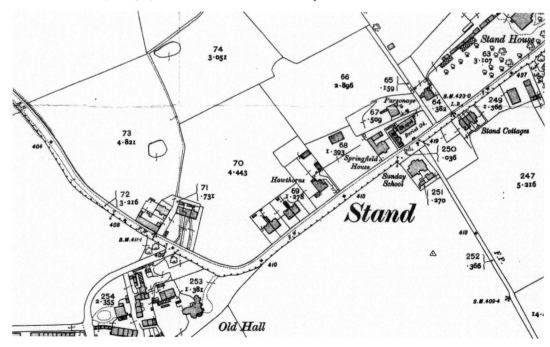